FINDING YOUR GOD-MATE!

ANTHONY GREVE

AND

SARAH MYERS-GREVE

Print ISBN: 979-8-9906565-3-6
E-Book ISBN: 979-8-9906565-2-9

Acknowledgments

We want to acknowledge all of our family, pastors, and friends for being there for us throughout our engagement, marriage, and ministries.

A special thank you to Evangelist Debra George for allowing God to use her outreach to bring us together and continue to support and love us!

Each one of you mean so much to us.
We would not be who we are without you!

Dedication

This book is dedicated to Matt and Susan Pinter.
Thank you for being columns and pillars in our lives.
Thank you for being family and for giving us your
unconditional love and support, as well as for praying us
into each other's lives. And thank you for saving
our marriage before it started. We honor you.

Contents

Foreword

Anthony and Sarah are world-changers and history-makers. Together they are impacting their world for Christ Jesus and living their dream! Before they met, Anthony was on a Philadelphia outreach with me and I had just met beautiful Sarah and had invited her to come, too! As we all walked the streets of the largest open-air drug market in America, God was working on something far greater, a union between two amazing people, Anthony and Sarah. They met, they fell in love and are now the perfect example of what it means to wait until you meet your God-mate. They both waited. However, they were not looking for a mate. The two of them were pursuing their God-given purpose of reaching the hurting when they both collided with their destiny. Anthony and Sarah were fulfilling God's calling as single individuals when they met. They have a beautiful love story and are role models of how God can take two lives that are surrendered to Christ and blend them into becoming *one*. This book will strengthen your waiting or your marriage and will bring hope and healing to all areas of your life.

Debra George
DebraGeorge.org

ONE

Starting Over

■ SARAH MYERS-GREVE

Start overs are some of the hardest moments in our lives. We have to look at the ruins of the life we had and figure out where to go from there. For me, my start over led me to Louisiana Adult and Teen Challenge, a 12-month-long drug rehabilitation and discipleship center. I was a convicted felon with a mustard seed of faith. But faith has been proven to rebuild Nations and restore lives. Faith was all I had left and it was all I needed. My friend, as you read our story, faith is all you need.

I sat in class listening and watching as the Directors of Louisiana Adult and Teen Challenge shared their hearts about waiting for the one God has for you. I pondered in my heart if it was possible for me to have the kind of spouse they were describing. I had grown up in a very dysfunctional home, so I wasn't completely sure of what a Godly family or husband looked like. I had never been in a healthy family setting. I had become very independent, and it had taken me years to get away from the destructive relationships that I had broken away from. After being in Teen Challenge for 7 months at this time, I had been going through the process of overcoming a 12-year-long drug addiction and many abusive relationships. I was wounded and hurt, still so much healing to go through. Yet my mind and heart was still thinking about that dream guy — the one who would one day walk into my life and sweep me off of my feet. I would daydream about the days to come and what life would be like.

Even though I had experienced many broken relationships I had a mustard seed of hope that one day I would have the man that God had for me. My hope at this point mainly came from the leaders of the program that I was in; they had set standards for themselves and gave us examples on what a godly marriage looked like. Ultimately, they had paid the price and waited for the one God had for them.

So many thoughts would go through my head, "How will I know how to pick the right one? Will it take me a full year or many years? Will he accept me with my past?" I had a lot of questions, and the reality was that my story of healing was just beginning.

You see, prior to my healing journey the kind of person I picked to be in a relationship with mirrored myself. I picked the person I was. They resembled me in every way; spiritually, emotionally, and physically. They would be addicted, wounded, and wandering through life. Those were the ones that seemed familiar and comfortable.

Not good, just comfortable.

Oftentimes when you are wounded and hurting, you will attract that same person. You find comfort in knowing they understand you. In the absence of Christ, that is your comfort factor. When I met Jesus in my jail cell and started walking with Him, over time He became everything I was looking for in the other person. I didn't even realize I was idolizing my relationships and trying to place the other person within the hole in my heart where only Jesus belonged.

When Jesus does not sit on the throne of your heart, someone or something will! It is either a man, yourself, your children, or your job. If it is not Jesus, then someone or something will reside as the king of your heart. And you will show your affections to that person or thing as though it deserves all of you when truthfully, you were created to give that part of your heart and affection to the King of Kings, Jesus. Place the King where He belongs, and you will find the one God has for you! He will fulfill you like nothing else and then lead you to the one.

So here I sat with broken relationships, wounded, and separated from my children for years. I had encountered tremendous loss, no home, and was facing years of probation. Now as a student in Teen Challenge, I was listening to a class about waiting on the person God has for you. I was starting life over at 25. What a humbling experience. But one thing was for sure, I had the most important thing right. I had accepted Jesus into my heart in a 5 x 9 cell (Get the book *3 Days in a Haze* to read Sarah's story) and encountered peace for the very first time in my life. He was now sitting on the throne of my heart and that, I knew, was the best "start over" a girl could have.

So, if you find yourself in the middle of a "start over" be encouraged with Jesus it can be the best thing that could have ever happened! Start overs can be where beauty comes from the ashes of the ruins of your life.

TWO

Become the One

SARAH MYERS-GREVE

Any time God has a promise for you, there is always a counterfeit. The Bible says in 2 Corinthians 11:14 KJV, "And no marvel; for Satan himself masquerades as an angel of light." An angel of light is something that presents itself as the promise but is not it at all. The angel of light has an agenda to get you to settle so that you will not reach your God-mate and destiny. The angel of light looks like something good but in itself really wants you to be destroyed. I believe God wanted us to know through this scripture that the enemy is a deceiver and very manipulating. The enemy is always dressed up to trick you. He doesn't play fair, and he uses your desires against you.

In my waiting, I had to refuse to settle. There were many counterfeits that presented themselves as men of God walking in their calling. I thought that they were my husband

5

from the Lord. The enemy got pretty crafty with his attempts to trip me up, but God was always contending for me to see the truth and not settle for the lies. The Lord was always revealing my worth to me and how I deserved God's best for my life. You deserve God's best for your life! Now, that doesn't downplay the men that I met along the way, it is just to say that God had specific plans and His best for my life. He has a best plan for everyone, just like it says in Jeremiah 29:11 NIV, "For I know the plans I have for you," declares the LORD, "plans to prosper you and not to harm you, plans to give you a hope and a future."

God has a good plan for all of us, we just have to trust and seek Him with all of our hearts.

The desires of the flesh will absolutely get you in trouble. The flesh is impatient and lustful. It must be crucified and submitted to the Lord, or you will be led by your flesh into situations that will derail you from the true purpose and will of God for you, especially in this area. Who you marry is the second biggest decision of your life after receiving Christ.

There were many practical things I had to do along the way while waiting for the one, including not getting caught by the counterfeits traps. I had to speak recorded prayers into my phone, saying out loud, "God, I thank you that you are not a man that you should lie, and you will fulfill what you promised. I thank you, God, that the man you have for me is real and that you are bringing him to me." I would pray that God would make me into someone who could be trusted with a man's heart and that God would make him into a man who could be trusted with mine.

During my seven years of waiting, I decided I would walk through every layer of healing that I could. I went through inner healing, counseling, deliverance, forgiveness, leadership courses, weight training, and many more personal development classes as well as weekend revivals. I knew if I kept pursuing God our paths would meet. I also came to understand that oftentimes in life, you will draw people who are like you. Some deliverance ministers call it familiar spirits. Well, I sure did not want anything familiar from my past, so I started to develop into a different person. I wanted to become the person I wanted to marry.

It is not enough to expect greatness out of someone else and then settle for ordinary yourself!

So, you must become the one! Begin to pursue your passion and find out things about yourself that have been hidden and need healing. You were never intended to hide your pain. Instead, pull back the curtain, expose it, and heal from it, so that it doesn't show up later on in your marriage, career, your ministry, etc. You will only be able to mask the pain of the past for a short amount of time, and then what's beneath the surface will make its way to the top. It is always the case because what is inside of you will always come out. In Proverbs, it says that *everything in life flows from the heart.*

I really desired a husband, but yet didn't even know what kind of a husband I wanted. The entire time that I was focused on wanting a husband, the Lord was trying to get me to focus on myself, and to become the person I wanted to marry. I am sure glad now that He did not give me the version of myself at that time!

Are you willing to become the person you want to marry? Are you willing to focus on becoming the one instead of falling for the counterfeits?

THREE

Make the List

■ SARAH MYERS-GREVE

Make a list and check it twice. Write out 35 qualities and 10 deal breakers of the things you desire to have in the man or woman that God has for you (you'll find this at the back of this book). Take some time to write them out. The deal breakers will guide you when your emotions are trying to get you involved with someone who is not from the Lord. Your desires will get more specific the longer you wait. During my waiting season, I wrote three to four lists out and then I got serious and specific because I was no longer willing to play games about what I was believing God for. I got focused and intentional with my list and prayers. You must be focused and intentional!

You see, when you begin to write out your list and envision what is in your heart coming to reality it becomes faith. You begin to see and believe in what is not there yet. It is the work of faith, and without works faith is dead. You must begin to work your faith in this area until you have plowed and prayed for your harvest to come. Even now, are you able to envision the man that God has for you? Do you really know the specifics? If you don't know, then you must begin to think, pray, and ponder on this and then begin to write down the vision!

Anything that God does in the natural always starts in your spirit and then comes out with a vision and a piece of paper. A list will help you see where you're going, and the list will guide you when you're lonely.

When we are lonely, our feelings guide us and can be the deciding factor if we allow them. When you have a list and deal breakers, you will know when red flags appear. The deal breakers were actually more helpful to me than the other things on the list because they helped me to know immediately when the red flags appeared so as not to ignore them.

After waiting as long as I did, I was unwilling to look over red flags because I was lonely. After a certain amount of time and experience, you will no longer play games with the red flags, you begin to take them seriously. These things appear to warn you.

Oftentimes, God shows us the red flags or the warnings in life in general, but it then becomes our responsibility to listen and follow. Just like when you're a teenager and you grow up and wish you had listened to your parents, it is the same way with God. If you do not listen to the warnings or the red flags you will wish you had. Dating or marrying the wrong person can really bring destruction upon your life, so it is vital to not ignore the red flags. Pray through them and bring them to counsel in your life. It is better to find out and make the break now than to marry the wrong person and walk through tragedy later on in life.

NOTE: DON'T SETTLE

FOUR

He is Real

■ SARAH MYERS-GREVE

After waiting for five years, I started to doubt if "the one" was really out there. Because of the thoughts of doubt that would come, I began to lose hope in my promise. So, I decided to take action by praying for the one God had for me. I had to start confessing what I wanted to see happen. The Bible says to speak a thing as though it is even when it's not!

So, I took this literally and would be driving down the road and I would begin to record prayers in my phone, confessing out of my mouth, "I know that who God has for me is real because God is not a man that He would lie." The truth is, after waiting for so long your belief can grow cold. The way I learned to continue to believe is to repeat the things that I knew to be true so that my heart and mind would be lit on fire with belief again. I specifically felt like

13

reminding myself repeatedly that, "The one God has for me is real!" Sometimes I would say this repeatedly many times a day. Then I would begin thanking God that the man He had for me was coming and that God was protecting him and guarding him from temptation.

Did you know the things you confess out of your mouth, you believe? You must change your confession to align with the things you want to see happen in your life! The Bible does say that the power of life and death is in the power of the tongue.

In the middle of my praying for my God-mate, the Lord started preparing my heart for the fulfillment of the promise through confirmations, signs, and words of knowledge through other believers. Although it wasn't for two more years that I would meet my husband, praying for him was a key part of my waiting and not settling for the counterfeit. As I prayed for my God-mate, my spirit got stronger with the understanding that everything that is in God's timing is the best for my life.

FIVE

In the Field

■ SARAH MYERS-GREVE

The year before I met my husband, I heard the Lord speak to me. He said, "Your husband will be a kinsman redeemer, like Boaz." The Lord showed me I would meet him in the field like Ruth did her Boaz. For me, that meant in the ministry field. I was directing a recovery ministry and doing outreaches mostly, so I knew God would bring him to me in those fields.

However, I stopped looking and just started working the fields. The harvest was in front of me and if I was pursuing God's work and way then I knew one day I would look up in the field and there my kinsmen redeemer would be. My redeemer of all those terrible relationships. My one that reflected the image of Christ. I stopped thinking "Could this be the one?" and just realized that the one would come for me when it was God's timing.

I kept walking into the fields God was calling me to work in and I kept listening to His voice and leading. I realized how in control God was of my life. After waiting for so long, you make a decision not to settle and just to trust that God will do it or He won't. Something settles inside of you to rest in the Lord's power to bring the promise to pass. I would tell God, "If others can have it, so can I. I will trust you to bring him." Now don't get me wrong, I did have many terrible dating experiences. Actually, the more dates I went on the worse they got. These dates lead me to surrender even more so to God's timing. I would tell myself, "Just focus on the field and God's special one will come!"

In the midst of my working the field, I was invited to hear a woman speak at a local church. I had heard rumors about this woman single-handedly shutting down strip clubs with Jesus, so I really wanted to go and hear her speak. Her name was Debra George. She was an Evangelist. So, I went for the weekend and the woman shared so many powerful testimonies about the places she would go and how she would see God move. During her third service, she mentioned God taking her to many states but suddenly I heard her say "Philadelphia". When she said that, I heard the Lord repeat the state in my spirit. I knew immediately that God was calling me there.

After service, the women in the program I was directing called me over to meet Ms. Debra George. As we connected, I shared with her that God was calling me to go with her to Philadelphia. She handed me her cell phone number and told me to call her but instructed me that I was the only one to come. Philadelphia is a dangerous city to go on a mission trip to because of the drugs and violence. Ms. Debra knew it was not for the common person but only for someone called by the Lord. She told me if I was to come that I must come alone and that I had to believe God to provide for me because their Airbnb was full with her other team. I said, "Yes ma'am." If God was calling me to come, He would provide.

The next morning, I received a message from one of my donors that they were sending me a special check to go on a special mission trip or whatever God was calling me to do. My Spirit jumped with excitement, and I immediately messaged Debra George letting her know. She said, "Pack your bags, we leave in two weeks."

NOTE: GO GET TO WORK IN THE FIELD!

SIX

Who Are You?

■ SARAH MYERS-GREVE

You must recognize the person by the Spirit, not the flesh. After I arrived in Philadelphia, I was in great anticipation of what God was going to do on this trip. I came to learn and serve. I came to be obedient to the Lord's voice because He was calling me to come. I was so thankful that this mighty woman of God allowed me to join her and her team.

The week before, the enemy was trying to attack me with anxiety and fear and cause me not to go. But I knew I had to be obedient to the Lord's voice, so I went and stayed with a friend where we prayed together, ate together, and worshipped together. The power of agreement broke the enemy's attack.

After arriving, I met Debra's team at a local outreach church for service where I was greeted and walked to the front of the church to sit with her team. Ms. Debra George greeted me with love and welcomed me in. We worshipped that morning and prayed for God's empowerment to fight the enemy's stronghold of heroin and addiction in Allegheny Ave., Philadelphia and other places that were ridden with drugs for miles and miles. We were in the worst heroin district in the nation. But God's light shines brightest in the darkest places.

As we prepared for service, we started praying over the things we would give away and then we headed for the streets. My training was short and sweet: follow them, listen, and then do! As I walked with them through this zombie land, my heart broke for the people. I watched as Debra George climbed into a tent to hug a woman who wouldn't wake up because she was passed out on heroin. She woke her up and the woman received prayer and Jesus!

After watching this happen a few more times I hit the ground running. That day we led over 60 people to Jesus. It was a glorious outpouring of God's love and protection.

Close to the end of the day, there was a girl I encountered named Felicia. She had only been out there three to four days. As I started ministering to her, one of the other team members spoke to me and said, "Hurry, there's a man coming toward us who is growling." So, I began ministering to the woman as he prayed against this growling man. This man had a demon and was trying to attack us and scare us off. However, the other team member prayed and commanded the demon to leave while I was ministering to Felicia. The demon-possessed man went away but then quickly five more just like him came after us. Suddenly, I heard the Lord say, "I will confuse your enemies." I also heard the Lord say that I should grab candy out of our candy bag and start handing it to them. People on heroin love candy. This candy was the thing that caused the enemy to get confused. And then suddenly, we were able to gain control over the situation. Within two minutes, me and the other team member had won all five of those men to the Lord! It was a powerful moment! After the men walked away, I turned and looked at the team member I had been ministering with. His name was Anthony. Suddenly, I looked into his eyes and felt such a respect for him. I said to myself, "Who are you? I think I have known you my entire life." I knew this was going to be a lifelong friendship, but I had no idea I had just met my Boaz in the field.

It wasn't until after I returned home from the mission trip when he began messaging me and updating me about the trip that we connected and stayed connected.

He offered to pray with me throughout the week and we talked about the Lord but never really about anything else. He was trying to get to know me in the Lord and how I felt about praying and my beliefs. He was such a gentleman.

It wasn't for a full month of praying that he actually asked me out.

It was such a beautiful, pure thing! The person God has for you will respect you and not push themselves on you. And one thing the Lord showed me after we met in Philadelphia was what God has for you will be birthed in the Spirit and not in the flesh. Our meeting was not fleshly or lustful. It was full of the Spirit of God and pure. I had such a reverence for him — like he was my best friend and someone very important in my life.

When you meet the one, you will know it by the Spirit of God, not by the flesh! Wait for the one!

SEVEN

The Single Life

■ ANTHONY GREVE

What do you do while waiting? The Single life is a very interesting period of time in a person's lifetime. It's a time when we are able to devote more of our time to prayer, to fasting, to reading, to studying the Word, and to serving the Kingdom.

But it is also the time when we find ourselves praying for the individual, the partner that God has for our lives. So, the season of serving also becomes your greatest season of waiting. A waiter is someone who serves people. In your season of waiting, be serving. Serving is the key to your future. The key to what you may ask? Serving is the key that unlocks the doors to your destiny, for opportunities, and to divine relationships, including the one whom you will marry. Many dread the single life but it is only because they don't understand their season. Your period of singleness is an opportune time to grow. It is what seems to be a desert season, but it is the greatest season of grooming and preparation for your life. Many want an incredible Kingdom spouse but fail to become that themselves. You must become the very thing that you believe in. Your season of waiting, the single life, must also be your time and season of preparing. Become who you would want to marry.

The single years are a special time because it is a set-apart time. It's a time you won't get back. Not that I would ever desire to go back, but don't rush the moment and the season that you are in. Take advantage of it and make the most of it. Most of the time, when the season is rushed, the mate becomes compromised. Meaning, you settled for less than God's best for your life, because you did not take the time to become developed and to become all that God had for you to be. Many want someone amazing without ever making the investment to become greater themselves. Make the most of being single. It's a time of intimacy between you and the King. It's a one-on-one lifestyle. You will learn the voice of God in your life and grow into the godly person that God has designed for you to be.

Take a note of this next nugget and write it down, you cannot skip the process. If you skip the process, you will only be robbing yourself of the best future that God has for you. You are in this season of singleness because God has something to teach you. You are in process. Your single life is not forever; it's just for right now. Take advantage of the time to pray, to minister, to travel, and to freely serve the Kingdom of God in your Single life, while God prepares you for the life to come because the life to come will no longer be you alone. It will be a merging where the two now become one. Two lives merge to become one life. Note that in that season there will be a death, a dying to yourself, where you will grieve being single. Not because a relationship is bad, but because you can now never go back to who you used to be. You must move forward in the things that God has for your life.

When my wife and I started dating, it was truly wonderful, but it was also very hard. Hard in the sense that we both had our own way of doing things, our own way of living, and our own way of thinking. I had been single for a very long time. I had tried to date on several occasions, but it just didn't work out, not because it was bad, but because it wasn't what God had for my life. You are pursuing what God has for your life. Don't settle for "OK" when you are seeking God for His best. If you were in a recent relationship that didn't work out, it doesn't mean that the individual was bad, sometimes it's just not what God has for you, and you have to let it go. Because I had been single for ten years and spent the last of those several years living back at home with my family and cat, I had developed a life and a routine that was fit for me.

Let me rephrase that, it was fit for the single me. I don't really like change. Though I knew it was good and knew beyond a shadow of a doubt that this was who God had for me, it didn't necessarily make the change any easier. Don't think that you'll know that it's God by how smooth things are. That is not always the case. You have to know the voice of God and what He said, because challenges come to all relationships. You can't make a decision based off a fleshly emotion. You must know the voice of God for yourself. If you are in a relationship for a long period of time, and there are no issues, I would begin to question things. Bumps in the road are absolutely normal and OK. You are trying to work it out and you are learning to adapt and to grow into and with someone else. Hard times are normal, truly.

I remember God speaking to me one day because I looked up to Him in the course of my wife and I dating and I said, "God, this is hard. I'm not sure that I can do this."

His response was, "Both marriage and singleness require a cross, which cross do you want?"

It was true. The cross of singleness can be celibacy and even lonely at times because we were created for relationships. As God says in Genesis 2:18 NIV, "…It's not good for man to be alone…" We weren't designed to be alone, and that's why loneliness hurts. That's why it becomes a cross and a choice.

The Apostle Paul chose singleness in order to fully serve the Kingdom and carry out his mission (1 Corinthians 7:7). Remember, this was a choice, not a requirement or obligation. You aren't holier because you decided to stay single.

And yet, marriage requires a cross because marriage is a sacrifice. You are no longer living for yourself, you are now living to care for someone above yourself and put them first. We are called to love our wives in the same way that Christ loves His Church. Ultimately, whether you remain single for the Kingdom or choose to marry and serve the Kingdom of God with a partner, both lifestyles will require a cross because though both lifestyles are very different, they both require sacrifice.

So, while you are living the single life, take this time to really press into God, because I know, being single is not easy, but know that your season is a blessing. It's not forever, it's just for right now. Take advantage of this time and make the most of it. Your seasons of preparation are usually the hardest because they are preparing you for the greatest. But you can know this, the harder the season, the greater the blessing that's coming.

So don't you dare coast in the waiting.

This is not a time for coasting, it's a time for growing. Let God develop you in this season of singleness. I cannot stress this point enough. Serve and love God with everything you have, because when God brings you the person that you've been waiting for, it's going to be absolutely marvelous.

EIGHT

Dating is Hard

■ ANTHONY GREVE

Waiting is hard, but ending up with the wrong person is harder. How do we find the right person? Who is the right person? Is there a right person for me? Can I date just anybody? We've all had to ask ourselves these very same questions in the midst of our search. How do we find the right person?

I know this, that finding the right person is critical. It may be the difference between life or death with your relationship with God, or the call of God on your life! See, you are called, so you can't just settle for anyone. Your God-mate has to be the mate that the King ordained for you, because no one else will do. You'll sell out just to settle into a mundane life that you were never called to and live in a constant state of wondering why nothing is working or where you went wrong. The truth is, dating can be hard, but soul-tying yourself to someone who is not connected to God's destiny for your life is way harder. The person you marry is going to be the person that you walk your God-given destiny with. It doesn't mean everything will always be easy, but you do need to know that it is God.

One of the ways to find God's mate for your life is through prayer, and two, making a list. If you don't know who or what you are looking for, you'll never know what to look for. You need to make a list (as prepared for you in the back of this book) as to what you want in a mate, what your personal desires are, what Kingdom attributes you're looking for, and what the deal-breakers are. If you have those things written out, it makes it easier to identify what you're looking for. So, make your God list, and be someone who refuses to settle!

As I tried dating throughout my Christian walk, I made a lot of mistakes. Mistakes in the sense that I was looking for what I wanted in the flesh, and not what was necessarily spiritually valuable, or even critical for that matter. So don't get caught up in the wrong things!

There were times that I tried to date throughout my Christian walk all while knowing that the person wasn't where they needed to be with God, but the problem was that I thought I could shape them. I thought that I could mold them. I thought that I could make them into what I wanted them to be in order for them to fit the call of God on my life and that which I was looking for. In other words,

I thought that I could help them become holier than they were, so to speak. Don't date someone with the intention of changing them! You need to date the person that God leads you to or brings into your life and you need to learn to love them where they are and for who they are, because the truth is, once you marry, it's almost like starting over. The two become one and you are learning to do life with this individual, all over again.

In other words, neither one of you is perfect, but you are committing to a journey that you will walk and grow in together. You can't make your Kingdom-mate; they must be found. And the truth is that the waiting is and can be hard! You'll even begin to wonder at times if the person that God has for you exists or not. But as I have seen in my life and the lives of many, over and over again, they do.

They exist.

You need to take this time of singleness for God to work out of you what He wants and for Him to prepare you for the marriage that He has for you. God really, absolutely, does have that perfect someone. And if you'll hang in there, like we have, and get to a place where you refuse to settle, that person will come!

I had got to a place and point in my life where not only was I not finding "The one" that God had for me, but I couldn't get a date at all, to the point where I actually thought it was concerning. I even said out loud to God, "God, something is wrong." I even told God that I was going to prove to Him that something was wrong. My idea of proving to God that something was wrong was by signing up for dating websites, just to see if I could get a date at all!

Truthfully, this was probably wrong. I was getting so weary of waiting and so concerned that I couldn't get a date that I signed up for not only one dating website but three! Do you know what happened? Nothing! Not one person was interested. There was one lady who wanted to talk to me about Biblical history, and that was about it.

I said, "You see, I told you that something was wrong God!" I knew it! But when I met my wife, something incredible happened. She shared with me what she had been believing in. She even had recorded prayers and had written down exactly what she had been praying for, AND IT WAS ME! It described me to a T. Someone who was an evangelist, sweet-spirited, kind, and even someone who spoke in tongues. One of the things that she prayed for was for God to block me from any counterfeits! She blocked me. Her prayers blocked me from being able to date anyone else. You can do this? Absolutely. According to your faith, you shall receive what you believe and ask for. I thought that her prayers had blocked me, but looking back in hindsight, they protected me. Even now, you need to begin to pray for the person that God has for your life.

NINE

Know What You Want

■ ANTHONY GREVE

If you don't know what you want, you won't know what to look for! In order for you to know what you're looking for, you must know who you are, and who you are in Christ. The reason people settle for anything is because they don't know themselves.

When you begin to understand your own worth and value, you won't settle for anything less than God's best for your life. You must know who you are, what you believe, and what you don't believe. You need to know what your convictions are and what your moral stances are. You need to know where you stand with the Bible. Do you believe in the baptism of the Holy Ghost? If you believe in speaking in tongues and your spouse doesn't, for example, you are going to run into issues! There are certain areas you will grow together in life, but there are some areas where you'll have to already know where you stand. If you don't, you're headed for a life of trouble. If you don't know what you believe, or who you are, you'll settle for anyone and anything. Singleness is not just a time to wait, it's a time for you to discover you. It's a time where you need to invest in self and self-growth. It's a time to press into healing from wounds and trauma, and as you begin to discover who you are in Christ, you'll know what you are looking for, in Christ.

In the waiting, know this, what you desire will change! And this is why it's important to make a list and place the vision of what you are looking for before you. That means to keep it before you continuously. My list from the time I got saved to when I met my wife ten years later had changed drastically because my priorities had changed. Who I was changed! You'll be amazed at how much you will grow, change, and develop in 10 years! It's normal to change. It's healthy to change. It's expected that as we grow, we will change. So, my list changed. I realized before I met my wife that I couldn't be with someone complacent but that I needed to be with someone who knew who she was in Christ, and who had already answered and was walking in their God-given calling. I wanted a woman who was independent, who knew how to lean on God more than she leaned on me. I even added to my list that my wife would be blonde-haired, blue-eyed, and from Tennessee! My buddy Travis can confirm this! Would you know, that's exactly what I got! You will get what you pray and believe God for! Oh, and I made sure to add to my list that she was a fire-filled woman of God, filled with the Holy Ghost! She was a tongue-talking fiery preacher, and I wouldn't settle for anything less. God did it. Not only did God do it, but God did the impossible in both of our lives by bringing us together. You'll read more on that soon! You can know this friend, if God did it for us, He will do it for you.

Waiting can get hard, but I want to focus on that word for a moment, waiting. A waiter isn't someone who does nothing, but a waiter is someone who serves. As you wait for the one that God brings into your life, you need to be about the King's business. You need to be serving. Serve God. Serve your local church. If you don't have a local church, you need to plug into one. Too many people are waiting for the person who will complete them, but no person other than Christ can complete you. Only God can complete you. You aren't looking for your other half, you're looking for your other whole. So, it's in the waiting that you need to keep pursuing the heart of God unwaveringly. Don't waver. Stay connected to the source. Keep your heart connected to His heart. Make pursuing God not just something else that you do, but it needs to be the first thing that you do. It needs to be your priority. Matthew 6:33 NIV says, "But seek first his kingdom and his righteousness, and all these things will be given to you as well." That includes a spouse! Be someone who remains faithful and steadfast in pursuing the heart and the love of God. Make sure that He is, becomes, and remains your number one lover! The Kingdom needs to be number one in your life, and you need a spouse who has put God first. It doesn't mean that you won't face issues, but if God isn't in His rightful place, which is number one, expectations that only God can meet will be placed on you, and that's going to cause problems. Whoever it is that you choose to marry, God needs to be number one in their lives as well as yours. This doesn't just happen, but it happens intentionally. It is a choice. Don't wait till you're married to make Him number one (if you're already married, make Him number one). He needs to be number one now.

Although your list will change, there are some non-negotiables. One non-negotiable for me was having a Kingdom woman of God. What you need to grab a hold of is that you can be a Christian, and yet not be Kingdom-minded. They are not the same thing. I needed someone in my life who was Kingdom-minded and whose agenda was advancing God's Kingdom on the earth. It means that we live to advance His Kingdom on the earth. It's the number one priority for us individually, and together as a couple. So, you have to ask yourself, is this what I'm looking for in my spouse? And even ask the harder question, am I where I want to be yet because even in my own life remember, we are growing, changing, and adapting. Like me, as you wait on God to bring you the one that He has for your life, that list may very much change, and that's OK! Don't be afraid to change or of change. Don't be afraid to let go. Don't be afraid to see through a new Kingdom perspective. Many want increase and advancement but aren't willing to make the changes to see this happen. The truth is that change can be scary. But I'll say this, even going into our third year of marriage, I'm always looking to grow and be better. I'm even in a season now where I'm pursuing counseling. Not because anything is wrong but because I want to grow into becoming a better man and learn how to be the best father and husband that I can be. Don't be afraid to grow, and don't be afraid of change. Change may be the very answer that you are looking for. It may be the very thing that you need.

TEN

God Speaks

■ ANTHONY GREVE

Won't He do it! I remember when I got a friend request from my wife, of course, she wasn't my wife at the time. Matter of fact, we didn't even know each other at all. To me, it seemed as if it were a random request from a random person, so I went to her page to see if I knew her. I didn't seem to know her at all, at which point I was going to delete the friend request, but that's when I noticed that we had a lot of mutual friends. I was living in Michigan at the time but had been traveling to and doing quite a bit of ministry in Tennessee. So, we knew a lot of the same people in ministry. Realizing that, I decided I'd better accept her friend request and that it might be a ministry connection.

What a ministry connection it was!

When I accepted her friend request, I heard the Lord speak to me, "This is your wife."

I said, "God, you gotta be kidding me," meaning, up to that point I hadn't been able to get a date and now God was sending me my wife. I said to the Lord, "God, if this is who you have for my life, you are going to have to do it. I'm not going to message her." Because if it was God, I was going to set it at what seemed to me an impossible and supernatural standard. I just figured I'd never see her again. Remember, He's the God of the impossible, not what is possible. What is impossible with man, is possible with God. So, that was my request, if this was the woman that God had for my life, then He was the one who was going to have to bring us together. I must have forgotten I was dealing with God.

Several months later, I headed off on a mission trip to Philadelphia to serve on the streets with Debra George Ministries. We were headed to one of the worst heroin districts, definitely in the United States, maybe even the world. There were miles of young people lining the streets of Allegheny and Kensington shooting needles in their arms, their feet, even in their necks. They were shooting up wherever they could find a vein. This place had been nicknamed, "Zombie Land." I had been on several trips with Debra George Ministries up to this point. It was always an incredible honor serving her ministry, and such an adventure! You never knew what was going to happen. From deliverance on a sidewalk to the dead being raised on a bench, there was no shortage of situations. We saw God move in many miraculous ways. Halfway through this trip, a young woman joined up with our ministry team to be a part of outreach. I had heard she was from Tennessee, so upon meeting her, I asked if she knew Robin Nation who was the director of Women at the Well Ministries in Athen's Tennessee, which was a women's recovery and discipleship home. She said that she knew her, so I said we needed to get a picture to send to her! Robin Nation had me in to speak several times and had become a mother in the Lord to me. It was wild meeting someone else who knew Mrs. Robin all the way in Philadelphia. Sarah and I had the opportunity to minister together on the streets in Philly. It was a wild time! I remember absolutely loving her spirit and heart for street ministry and evangelism. She was just a very cool person. There were so many stories from those few days! Sarah didn't end up staying the entire trip, but I remember that after she left, thinking to myself, "This girl is really cool. This is someone I could be friends with, at least."

So, I decided to look her up on Facebook in order to stay connected. It popped up as we were already friends. *Wait, what?* How was that possible, I had never even met this person before, or so I thought. Well, when I clicked on her profile page it came up… that's right… you guessed it. It was the profile of the girl that God said was my wife. The one that I put a demand on God saying, "If this is who you have for me, you are going to have to do it, because I'm not messaging her." I share this with you for two reasons: One, because it's absolutely supernatural. That's how God operates. Two, because if God can do it for me, He can do it for you! Don't settle.

God knows how to connect the dots! No one is more in control than He is. He is the God of your destiny! He can and wants to get you to your God-mate. This is our story. God is going to give you your own! Ask Him for it. Sarah and I had both prayed for a God story in the way that we would meet our spouses. And He did it!

Even though I knew from that moment forward that she was my wife, I didn't just jump right out and say, "God spoke to me and said you were my wife!" Don't be that person. Even if God spoke it, don't blow it. Give things time to develop and give things time to unfold. I didn't say anything to Sarah, I just hid that word in my heart. For the first month of us knowing each other, dating wasn't even mentioned. We talked, got to know each other, and prayed together almost daily.

After about a month, I asked her if she knew. She said, "Call me." From there we both talked about dating. Another confirmation for us was that we had both been featured on CBN's 700 Club! (our testimonies). Ask God for confirmation. Matter of fact, it would be silly not to! One of the biggest confirmations for Sarah was a yellow butterfly. In that very first picture we took together in Philadelphia, she later noticed that on the fence behind us in the photo was a large yellow butterfly. God isn't afraid of our asking for Him to confirm His will, matter of fact I think that He enjoys it because, in the discovery of God's will, we discover Him. It was from that point on we began to date.

ELEVEN

Coming Together

■ ANTHONY GREVE

The dating season began. But before I get into this chapter, let me say this, too many people are more concerned about finding the one than becoming the one. The truth is that you will attract who you are. So, in the waiting, you must be becoming.

The bottom line is, dating can be difficult. It's a season of getting to know one another. And fellas, let me say this, "Save sex for marriage." That goes for you too ladies. Because if they don't end up being the ones that you marry, then you take something from someone that doesn't belong to you. Men, she doesn't need to see that you can have sex with her, she needs to know that you can be committed to her. You are called to love and be there for her. Sex is the act that consummates a marriage union. When people say things like, we are just friends of benefits, it is a straight-up anti-God assault on what God ordained and created. Sex was created for marriage, period. She needs to see you're committed. No marriage, no sex. Dating is the time for you to get to know one another. Meet in public settings. Don't date in secret where you are going to constantly be tempted. For accountability purposes, I let the people in my life know that we were dating: my family, and my pastor. If you are too embarrassed to bring them around your family, church family, or pastor, that is your first red flag. Get out of it while you can. If you are afraid to bring them to church because your church is a little more radical, then it's probably not someone that you are equally yoked with and should be dating. The point is that dating is the season of learning about each other and discovering whether this is the person that God has for you. There were times when I had to fight and labor in prayer for the relationship because I knew beyond a shadow of a doubt that this was who God had for my life. You have to assess what is a red flag and what is a fear. Many times, people break it off out of fear. There were several times when my now wife and I had to push through fears while we were dating. There were even times when we didn't know how we were going to make it work. Keep in mind that this was also a long-distance relationship. We traveled back and forth between Michigan and Tennessee as we dated. But when you know that it's the one that God has for you, you learn how to work through those things. Dating can be scary, so date in the light. If you don't feel comfortable being alone, bring accountability. And again, remember, difficulty doesn't mean that it's the wrong person. It may be that God is trying to work something out of you. I had been single for so long that it was hard for me to let someone in and surrender my own way of doing things. For years as a single man, life was about my shoes, my closet, my car, and my cat. But marriage is about the surrender of your own life to another.

Coming together is a process. God said that the two shall become one. One of the things that we've learned is that there is an initial coming together in the wedding ceremony and consummation, but that's not really the coming together. Some couples marry but never come together. The coming together is the continual process of the two lives becoming one. The first two years of our marriage was the working out of ourselves. It's a continuous process of unification. It's a work that God does in us. It is not a one-time event. So, know that the process of becoming one is something that God will continue to knit together over time.

One day I said to Sarah, "I think the Lord said that we're supposed to get married in July." At this time, that was only a few months away and we hadn't been dating very long. My statement stunned her because not long before we met, the Lord told Sarah that she would be married by July. She didn't know how that would be possible because at that point she wasn't even dating anybody, but as an act of faith, she wrote on her calendar in the month of July, "Get married." This was such a beautiful confirmation for us.

I said, "Did we just get engaged?" We were engaged before we were engaged! Since we were already planning a wedding, I felt it only fitting to get her a ring. I purchased her a beautiful Vera Wang ring and proposed to her, just the two of us, on the beautiful beach of Lake Michigan. Honor her request. Sarah doesn't like to be the center of attention, so I certainly wasn't going to propose to her in front of a bunch of people. Know your partner! God will confirm the person to you every step of the way, including the right ring to get. The beauty of dating is if God confirms that it's not the person for you, you can break it off in a healthy manner. Sex creates soul ties that are much harder to break. Save yourself for marriage! And if it's God's will, He's going to confirm it every step of the way, just like He did for us.

Again, difficult doesn't mean it's the wrong person. Iron sharpens iron. Sometimes you don't even know the edges that you have that need to be sanded down until there is someone there to rub you the wrong way or to expose an area of your life in which you need healing. The pursuit of healing is something that we have kept in the forefront of our lives and our relationship. Let God work the hard things out. There was even a time when we were dating that I said to my friends Matt and Susan, "I don't know if I can do this," not because there was anything wrong with Sarah, but because it was just hard for me. I remember Matt asking, "Did God say this is the person you are supposed to marry? And if so, what reward is there in giving up?" You have to push through the hard times, because there is no reward in quitting!

TWELVE

Never Stop Dating!

■ ANTHONY GREVE

Continue to pursue each other no matter what! We were married on July 30, 2021, in Sparta, TN. We had a beautiful evening wedding at The Duck Pond Manor as the sun was going down with an incredible backdrop of the hills of TN. We were both surrounded by family and friends and had our dream wedding. It was such an incredible venue! What's even more incredible is that Debra George flew in to marry us. It was on a ministry trip to Philadelphia with Debra George that we first met. We had a Christian rapper, and it even ended up being an outreach wedding with an altar call. We also had a butterfly release as well as a sparkler exit. It was more than we could have asked for!

Sometimes we think that everything will perfectly come together, but that doesn't mean that you still won't have to fight for the promises of God in your life. And never stop contending for them! The Bible says that, *the violent take it by force*. Sometimes the blessings of God are simply released into our lives, and there are other times where we have to fight for our promised land.

Marriage for us has been absolutely incredible. It seems like we did more in our first two years of marriage than some do in a lifetime! We launched a house church, traveled the world, and even spent our one-year anniversary on Waikiki Beach in Honolulu, HI. A beautiful marriage doesn't just happen, a beautiful marriage is created and maintained. One key that I learned that you could apply to your own life is to never stop pursuing her! Keep pursuing each other. The pursuit doesn't stop when you get married, the pursuit is just beginning. Never stop dating your spouse. We date regularly and we have fun. Have fun y'all! Life is fun. It's meant to be enjoyed!

One night as we were walking into a restaurant my wife said, "Tonight we are going to be British," with a British accent and for our entire date we were only allowed to speak with a British accent. It was incredible because one of the owners came over to greet our table, and she was actually British! Have fun with your marriage. Laugh, date, go to the movies! Take vacations. Not every vacation has to be a big event! We're in Tennessee, so sometimes for us, a weekend getaway to the mountains will do just fine! The point is, that you can never stop pursuing each other. This is what will keep your love for one another burning and your marriage on fire, year after year.

And hey, when you're frustrated, take ten.

Go for a walk. Go spend some time in prayer. Put a covenant in place of what you are going to do when things get heated. If you don't have a plan, then you won't have a path to victory. Create a plan before problems occur!

Marriage has been a beautiful journey. This is just the beginning for you!

THIRTEEN

The King of Your Heart

■ SARAH MYERS-GREVE

The heart is that which enthrones what is most precious to you. And what is most precious to you is that which the mind seeks, and the emotions express (Matthew 6:21).

In other words, your heart values and worships what is most precious to you. We all have a throne in our hearts determined to take precedence in our lives. The thing that sits on the throne is the voice that will guide us and speak to us. When searching for your God mate, you must make sure that Jesus is on the throne of your heart above all other things, before you will ever meet your God mate.

All the way back to Genesis, God is a bringer of order. With God, He has a divine order of things for your life. He knows exactly in what order to bring your husband or wife. But the first rule of order is to make sure that God is first and Jesus has full rule and reign of your heart and life. It's all about Lordship and being willing to let Jesus be on the throne and rule over every other thing. He must rule over your friends, people's opinions, over going out to the bars on Saturday nights, and over your own pick of a mate for yourself.

We do at times believe we know what's best for ourselves so we make decisions without seeking the Lord. When we do this, it proves to the Lord that we are sitting on the throne of our hearts and not Jesus. In our own strength and in our own control we will receive a mate that we picked and not the Lord.

That leaves you with the question: Do you want to pick, or do you want God to bring you, His pick? I can testify you most certainly will want to wait on God's pick for your life because there is perfection inside God's will and ways. Yes, I said perfection! When you allow Jesus to be the King of your heart and stay on the throne, that's when God will bring you your God-mate. You will have to prove to the Lord that He can stay on the throne of your heart through the challenges that come, and there will be tests and challenges that make you stronger and keep you steady. This is the ultimate test of your heart because it's God's divine order. He comes first, and then you will be able to love your God-mate the way God always intended man and wife to love each other. As much as I want to say I love my husband and children, I can't say I love them more than God because God must come first in our life and only then we can love others correctly. Keeping this order keeps you from making people and things idols in your life. This order helps you to love others the way God does because He comes first and then flows through you showing you boundaries and when you have done all you can for someone. He shows you how to love past pain and how to not give up. It is His love you love with when He is the King of your heart and then everything else flows into the right place.

When Jesus is the King of your heart you can be trusted with the heart of the God-mate that has been picked for you. It is an act of trust in you from God. He is trusting you with His child's heart that He prepared for you to guard, protect, love, and encourage. When you understand this and keep Jesus the king of your heart, you will not be far away from the one God has for you! Tell yourself out loud, "I know the person God has for me is real because God is not a man that He should lie, and what He does for one He will do for another!"

The day we met

Our wedding day

35 Qualities

If you are reading this in e-book, you will need paper and a writing utensil for this next section.

Here are 35 spaces for you to fill in and list 35 qualities that you would like to see in your future spouse. If you are already married, you can list the qualities that you would like to see God develop in your spouse and then pray that list over them.

1. _____
   _____

2. _____
   _____

3. _____
   _____

4. _____
   _____

5. _____
   _____

6. _____
   _____

7. _____
   _____

8. _____
   _____

9. _____
   _____

10. _____
    _____

11. _____
    _____

12. _____
    _____

13. _____
    _____

14. _____
   _____

15. _____
   _____

16. _____
   _____

17. _____
   _____

18. _____
   _____

19. _____
   _____

20. _____
   _____

21. _____
   _____

22. _____
   _____

23. _____
_____

24. _____
_____

25. _____
_____

26. _____
_____

27. _____
_____

28. _____
_____

29. _____
_____

30. _____
_____

31. _____
_____

32. _____

_____

33. _____

_____

34. _____

_____

35. _____

_____

10 Deal Breakers

Here is a list of 10 deal breakers for you to fill out. These are 10 things that you will not compromise on in making the decision of your future spouse! In other words, if there is a deal breaker in their life that's on your list, you're gonna' know, they aren't the one!

1. _____
   _____

2. _____
   _____

3. _____
   _____

4. _____
   _____

5. _____
   _____

6. _____

_____

7. _____

_____

8. _____

_____

9. _____

_____

10. _____

_____

The next three pages are dedicated to you writing a letter to your future spouse. These are precious moments and pages that you'll one day be able to present to the spouse that you have waited for. Take your time and pray through as you write. While my wife and I were dating, I wrote 31 letters for her and presented them to her as a gift on our wedding day. Every so often she opens one and reads it. She still has yet to read them all! One day this letter will mean something so special to the one that you have waited and prayed for.

Maybe you are married but have never done something like this. We encourage to take the time to write a letter to your husband or wife and share with them just how much they mean to you. It will always be something to cherish. Begin your letter on the next page!

Letter to My Spouse

_____

_____

_____

_____

_____

_____

_____

_____

_____

_____

_____

_____

_____

_____

_____

_____

_____

_____

_____

_____

_____

_____

_____

_____

Prayer of Blessing

We pray that God blesses your union inevitably. Not only do we pray that He leads you to the right person that he has for you, but that your marriage would have on it unusual favor and grace. We declare that it would be abundant! That every need would be met and every desire of your heart fulfilled. We pray that your covenant will exceed your wildest dreams and expectations. We pray that it will be peaceful. We pray that you'll dance in the rain and soak in the sun and that you'll enjoy each other from your meeting point and always. We pray that you'll forgive often and that you will love more, and that there will be no end to what God does through your life. We also pray that together you will fulfill your calling and mandate as a couple and that you will discover your Kingdom purpose early on. May God shower you always with his blessing, favor, and His goodness.

In Jesus' Name, we pray,
Amen

Anthony and Sarah Greve

~ Numbers 6:24-26 ~

"The LORD bless you
and keep you;
the LORD make His face shine on you
and be gracious to you;
the LORD turn His face toward you
and give you peace."

More From
Anthony and Sarah

Anthony and Sarah are both ordained ministers of the Gospel. They are the CEOs of Anthony Greve Ministries and Invitation Ministries as well as having launched together, Global Lighthouse, which will rescue and house women as well as operate as a center for revival.

Other Books — Available on Amazon

Anthony Greve: *Delivered From Evil*
Sarah Myers-Greve: *3 Days in a Haze*

You can also visit Anthony and Sarah on the web.

Anthony Greve
www.anthonygreveministries.com

Sarah Myers-Greve
www.invitationministries.com

WE GREATLY THANK YOU
FOR YOUR SUPPORT!